TIMMY TALKS TAXES!

By: **Dre Mudaris**
Illustrator By: **Cameron Wilson**

ISBN: 9798358982697

Copyright © 2022 Children To Wealth

2

Reading Levels

Interest Level: K-Gr. 7	DRA Level: 24	Lexile Measure: 770L
Grade Equivalent: 3.7	Guided Reading: M	

WATCH ALONG
(SCAN CODE BELOW)

"What would you do If you ended up paying no taxes this year?"

Timmy's Father asks himself in the mirror as he gets ready to take Timmy to golf practice.

*It begins to thunderstorm

"Dad, did you hear that? Do you think I will still have practice today?"-Timmy asks.

"I'm not sure, son." -Timmy's father responds.

*Ding

*A text message is received on Timmy's father's phone. It reads, "Due to the inclement weather, practice is canceled."

"Welp, looks like practice has been canceled, son."-Timmy's father announces.

"Oh, okay. I was looking forward to it. Ah well. Can I hang with you?"-Timmy asks.

"Sure. I don't have a problem with that."-Timmy Father says.

"What do you have planned for today anyway?"-Timmy asks.

"Uncle Dre is going to be introducing me to one of his accountants today,"- Timmy's Father responds.

"I didn't know that it was tax time, Daddy. I thought you only see your accountant when it's tax time."-Timmy asks.

"That was my old ways, son but after speaking with Uncle Dre, I learned that tax preparation is just as important if not more than tax filing."-Timmy's father responds.

*Ding

*Another text message is received on Timmy's Father's phone.

"I'm Pulling up now."-Timmy's Father reads his text message out loud.

"Speaking of Uncle Dre, that him pulling into the driveway."
-Timmy's father says.

"Hooray!"-Timmy says as he opens the door.

"Hey guys!"-Uncle Dre says as Timmy opens the door.

"Hey, Uncle Dre, we were just speaking about you and how you introduced me to the idea of tax preparation."
-Timmy's father says.

"Why, of course. Preparation is always best in everything we do."-Uncle Dre responds.

"Do you see the accountant early to evade taxes, Dad."-Timmy asks.

"Oh no, no, no. Not evade, but avoid."-Timmy's Father says.

"Isn't that the same? What's the difference?"

Side Note

Tax Evasion- Tax evasion is an illegal attempt to defeat the imposition of taxes by individuals, corporations, trusts, and others.

Tax Avoidance- Tax avoidance is the legal usage of the tax regime in a single territory to one's own advantage to reduce the amount of tax that is payable by means that are within the law.

Tax Haven- A tax haven is a country or place with very low "effective" rates of taxation for foreign investors. ("headline" rates may be higher).

"That's a great question, Timmy."-Uncle Dre says as they leave the house and prepare to visit the accountant.

"Well, tax avoidance is legally arranging your tax affairs to ensure only the minimum amount of tax is paid."
-Uncle Dre says.

"Yes, Timmy, so the biggest difference is that Tax Avoidance uses legal methods of reducing taxable income or taxes owed..."
-Timmy's Father adds.

"Interesting. Are there any examples of these methods?"
-Timmy asks.

"Sure, there are,"-Uncle Dre says.

"This can be done by various allowed deductions, credits, write-offs, and also by using tax advantage accounts."
-Uncle Dre adds.

"Tax advantage accounts?"-Timmy questions.

"Yes, such as IRAs and 401(k) 's."
-Timmy's Father adds.

"Oh, I see now."-Timmy says.

"So, what is Tax Evasion"-Timmy asks.

"Well, Tax Evasion is the use of illegal methods of concealing income or information from the IRS."
-Uncle Dre answers.

Side Note

401(K)- A 401k is an employer-sponsored retirement account. It allows an employee to dedicate a percentage of their pre-tax salary to a retirement account.

IRA- An individual retirement account (IRA) is a tax-advantaged account that individuals use to save and invest for retirement

Capital Gains- Capital gain is an economic concept defined as the profit earned on the sale of an asset which has increased in value over the holding period.

Tax Allowances- An allowance is claimed for each qualifying situation that would reduce a taxpayer's taxable income, such as personal exemptions, child tax credits, or daycare expenses.

"Oh no. That doesn't sound good."-Timmy says, concerned.

"It isn't. Two words can simplify Tax Evasion. Lying and Hiding."-Timmy's Father says.

"Wow."-Timmy says.

"Wow, is right, and there are a lot of penalties that come along with Tax Evasion."-Uncle Dre says.

"Penalties? If I don't report my income or a fraction of my income, am I automatically a criminal? "-Timmy asks with surprise.

"That is another great question, Timmy."-Uncle Dre says.

"The answer is no. The IRS believes that intent is key. However, if you want to evade taxes, and that is your intent and the IRS can prove it, well then yes, you will be engaging in a criminal act."-Uncle Dre responds.

"Wow, this is so interesting. What are the possible penalties for evading taxes."-Timmy asks.

"Some of the penalties include but or not limited to, A felony on your record, five years in jail, a fine of up to $250,000 ($500,000 for corporations), and a bill for the cost of prosecuting you." -Uncle Dre responds.

"Oh No."-Timmy says again as they arrive at the accountant's office.

Side Note

IRS- The Internal Revenue Service (IRS) is the revenue service of the United States federal government, which is responsible for collecting taxes and administering the Internal Revenue Code, the main body of the federal statutory tax law.

Intent- Intent refers only to the state of mind with which the act is done or omitted. It differs from motive, which is what prompts a person to act or to fail to act.

"I will meet you guys there. Let me just find parking." -Uncle Dre says as he drops Timmy and his father off at the front of the accountant's office to go and park his truck.

"His name is Mr. Lee and he is expecting you two."-Uncle Dre yells from his window as he drives away.

"Mr. Lee. Got it."-Timmy's father says to himself as they proceed into the building.

"Hello, gentlemen. Right this way, Mr. Lee is expecting you."
-The secretary says to greet Timmy and his Father.

"Wow. I love this place."-Timmy's father says to Timmy
as he admires the paintings and designs of the building.

"Thank you, Vanessa."-Mr. Lee says to his secretary as he
prepares to greet Timmy and his Father.

"Good Afternoon, Gentlemen."-Mr. Lee says to Timmy and his Father.

"I assume Uncle Dre is parking that Truck of his."-Mr. Lee says.

"Yes, he sure is. How did you know?"-Timmy asks.

"Ever since I explained the tax advantage of buying a vehicle over a certain weight, Uncle Dre has been in love with his new truck."-Mr. Lee says.

"There are tax advantages when it comes to vehicles?" -Timmy's father says surprisingly.

"Hey guys, found perfect parking."-Uncle Dre says as he enters Mr. Lee's office.

"Perfect timing. I was just about to explain how you can use taxes regarding vehicles."- Mr. Lee says.

"Let me take a seat. I love this to hear about the 6,000-pound rule." –Uncle Dre says as he pulls up a chair to join Timmy and his father.

"6,000-pound rule? What is that?"-Timmy asks.

"Yes, well, the 6,000-pound rule states if your vehicle is over 6,000 pounds, you get to deduct 100% of that vehicle on your taxes.."

"This is interesting."-Timmy says.

"Yes, very much so. You also have the financing, leasing, and mileage methods."-Mr. Lee adds.

"Which method is most popular amongst your clients?" -Timmy's father asks.

"It varies based on the need and situation. But the most the important thing to understand is that when you purchase a vehicle for your business, regardless of the method you choose, the vehicle becomes an asset for the business and anytime you have any asset for your business you get to depreciate."

"What does 'Depreciate' mean, Mr. Lee."-Timmy asks.

"Well, When you deprecate any type of asset, you are allocating the cost of whatever asset you acquire, and you are writing it off over time." –Mr. Lee says.

"I was thinking of leasing a vehicle for my business."-Timmy's father says.

"Leasing is an option. Now with leasing, you get to write off 100% of the lease payment."-Mr. Lee says.

"Oh really, how about financing?"-Timmy's father asks.

"If you are financing and leasing, you can take deductions such as gas, insurance payments, registration, car washes, tires, and many more. This is because you get to write these things off. This is called the actual method"-Mr. Lee explains.

Side Note

6,000 Pound rule- Under the current tax law, vehicles with a weight of 6,000 lbs or more are exempt from annual depreciation caps. Section 179 (a) allows a taxpayer to elect to treat the cost (or a portion of the cost) of any § 179 property as an expense for the taxable year in which the taxpayer places the property in service.

Depreciation- Depreciation is the process of deducting the total cost of something expensive you bought for your business. But instead of doing it all in one tax year, you write off parts of it over time. When you depreciate assets, you can plan how much money is written off each year, giving you more control over your finances.

Writing off- A write-off is a reduction of the recognized value of something. In accounting, this is a recognition of the reduced or zero value of an asset. In income tax statements, this is a reduction of taxable income, as a recognition of certain expenses required to produce the income.

"What is the mileage method."-Timmy asks.

"With the mileage method, you just track your miles from all of your business activities throughout the year."-Mr. Lee says.

"Ok, I understand. But Can you use the mileage method and the actual method together?"-Timmy's father asks.

"No, you can not. You must take advantage of either the actual method or the mileage method. And remember, the actual method is writing off your expenses such as lease, insurance, etc., and the mileage method is a quick calculation." -Mr. Lee explains.

"How did this all start? When did we begin paying taxes in the first place?"-Timmy asks.

"Great question, well in 1943, during World War 2, the United States government passed the current tax payment act."-Mr. Lee says as Timmy grabs a notebook from his bag and begins to take notes.

"Sounds like the government needed money and tax revenue to fund the war."-Uncle Dre says as he stares out of the window.

"That is correct."-Mr. Lee says.

"What was life like regarding taxes before 1943?"-Timmy asks.

*Uncle Dre notices the rain has stopped and the sun is appearing behind the clouds.

"Before 1943, the government had to wait for taxpayers to pay their taxes. However, to solve this problem, the government passed the current tax payment act."-Mr. Lee says.

"And what did the current tax payment act do?"-Timmy asks.

"It allowed the government to get paid before the worker got paid."-Mr. Lee responds.

"Great question, well in 1943, during World War 2, the United States government passed the current tax payment act."-Mr. Lee says as Timmy grabs a notebook from his bag and takes notes.

"Interesting." -Timmy says as he continues to take notes.

"Yes, it is."-Mr. Lee says.

*Ding

*Timmy's father receives a text message.

"The rain has stopped, and we will be resuming practice in 2 hours."-Timmy's father reads aloud from his phone

"Yay! I get to have golf practice today."-Timmy says in excitement.

"It seems so."-Timmy's father responds.

"Perfect timing, I have to get ready for a meeting myself."
-Mr. Lee says.

"It was such a pleasure meeting you, Mr. Lee, and thank you Uncle Dre for introducing us. I want to set an appointment and prepare for this upcoming tax season." -Timmy's father says.

"The pleasure is all mine. How is Next Thursday?"-Mr. Lee says.

"That is perfect."-Timmy's father responds.

"Glad I can assist."-Uncle Dre says as they leave Mr. Lee's office.

References

Capital, S. (2021): *Mileage Log Book.*. New York, NY: Penguin Publishing

Daily, F (2008): *Tax Savvy for Small Business: A complete tax strategy.* Los Angeles, CA: California Press.

Dunshine, A. (2020): Book son Taxes for beginners. New York City, NY: Chronicle Books.

Guilda, N.. (2021): The book on Retirement. New York City, NY: Avery Trade.

Mackwani, A.. (2021): Tax Strategies for High Net Worth. New York City, NY: Avery Trade.

Terms of Use

All use of the *Timmy Talks Taxes book*, accessible at www.childrentowealth.com and related subdomains (collectively, the "Web site") is subject to the following terms and conditions and our Privacy Policy all of which are deemed a part of and included within these terms and conditions (collectively, the "Terms"). By accessing the book you are acknowledging that you have read, understand, and agree to be bound by these Terms.

These Terms represent a binding contract between you and *Mudaris LLC* (and any of their respective principals, officers, shareholders, members, employees or agents are herein collectively referred to as *"Children To Wealth"* or "we"). These Terms are in addition to any other agreements between you and Mudaris LLC. If you do not agree with any of these terms and conditions, please do not use this book.

Mudaris LLC reserves the right to change, modify, add or remove portions of these Terms at any time for any reason. Such changes shall be effective immediately upon posting. You acknowledge by accessing our book after we have posted changes to this Agreement that you are agreeing to these Terms as modified.

TRADEMARKS, COPYRIGHTS AND OTHER INTELLECTUAL PROPERTY

Visit ChildrenToWealth.com and view more books that you will Enjoy!

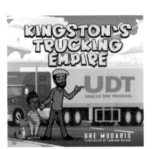

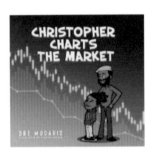

And Much More !!!

NOTES

_____

_____

_____

_____

_____

_____

_____

_____

_____